UP
FOR
SALE

HUMAN TRAFFICKING
AND MODERN SLAVERY

ALISON MARIE BEHNKE

TWENTY-FIRST CENTURY BOOKS / MINNEAPOLIS

names have been changed to protect an individual's privacy and safety. Whether the names are real or not, all the stories are true.

Twenty-First Century Books
A division of Lerner Publishing Group, Inc.
241 First Avenue North
Minneapolis, MN 55401 USA

For reading levels and more information, look up this title at www.lernerbooks.com.

Library of Congress Cataloging-in-Publication Data

Behnke, Alison.
    Up for sale / by Alison Marie Behnke.
      pages   cm
    Includes bibliographical references and index.
    ISBN 978-1-4677-1611-6 (lib. bdg. : alk. paper)
    ISBN 978-1-4677-4797-4 (ebook)
    1. Human trafficking—Juvenile literature. 2. Prostitution—Juvenile literature. I. Title.
    HQ281.B44 2015
    306.3'62—dc23   2013022607

Manufactured in the United States of America
1 – DP – 7/15/14

Contents

Chapter 1:
MODERN-DAY SLAVERY

Haitian *restaveks* are modern-day slaves. They are typically sent by their parents to work in another home because the parents cannot afford to support the child. The term *restavek* comes from the French words *reste avec,* which mean "to stay with."

Trafficking thrives in the shadows. And it can be easy to dismiss it as something that happens to someone else, somewhere else. But that is not the case. Trafficking is a crime that involves every nation on earth, and that includes our own.

—*Hillary Rodham Clinton, US secretary of state, 2009*

When Williathe Narcisse was nine years old, she left her home in Haiti and moved to Miami, Florida, with her employer Marie Pompee and Marie's family. Williathe was a Haitian restavek, an unpaid child servant. She had become enslaved at the age of six, when her mother died. When she got the chance to move to the United States with the Pompees, she hoped for new opportunities and a better life. Instead, Marie Pompee's son sexually assaulted Williathe, and the whole family punished her with beatings for tiny mistakes.

Many times Williathe wasn't even sure what she had done wrong. But it didn't really matter. She couldn't argue or fight back, or she would be punished more. So she tried not to make the Pompees angry and hoped that the next day would be better.

Williathe is not a character from the long-ago past. She is a real girl, who only gained her freedom in 1999. And she's not alone. She's one of the world's millions of victims of human trafficking—modern slavery.

VOICES OF THE VICTIMS: "T"

Withelma "T" Ortiz Walker Pettigrew—whom everyone calls T—had a difficult and dangerous childhood. Her parents, who were addicted to drugs, neglected her as a toddler. Eventually she was put into foster care, moving from home to home to home. Then, at the age of ten, T was trafficked into prostitution in Oakland, California. Her trafficker manipulated her feelings, promising to care for her—something she'd never known. But he beat her if she didn't bring home enough money.

When T was seventeen, social worker Nola Brantley helped her escape her trafficker. Since then, T has dedicated herself to helping other victims of trafficking. She is a board member of the human rights organization Rights4Girls, and she works with the Rebecca Project for Human Rights to push for greater focus on sex trafficking within the United States. T also mentors fellow survivors and speaks up on their behalf. She says, "My definition of freedom is deeper than most. For so long, my freedom was nonexistent. My every move was watched, my every conversation was observed. My clothing and food portions and options were at the mercy of another. Living in fear and terror . . . my physical self seemed to belong to everyone but me."

Slaves were common in ancient Rome. This ancient Roman mosaic in Piazza Armerina, Sicily, dates to the fourth century and depicts two slaves carrying a wild boar.

THEN AND NOW

When most people in the United States think of slavery, they think of the Atlantic slave trade of the 1500s. Slave traders of that era forcibly took local peoples from western Africa to European colonies and to settlements in the Americas and the Caribbean. Later, the young United States of America was home to many slaves.

But the history of slavery stretches back thousands of years to many other parts of the world, including the ancient kingdom of Mesopotamia (modern-day Iraq) and the empires of ancient Egypt, Greece, and Rome. Many slaves in these empires were captured in war and taken back to the lands of the conquerors to be servants and laborers. Similarly, in many parts of Africa, victors in ethnic conflicts often enslaved the losers. China, India, and other Asian countries also have histories of slavery stretching back many centuries. In northern Europe, the Vikings of the eighth through eleventh centuries also had slaves.

SLAVERY BY A NEW NAME

In modern times, slavery has a different face and goes by a different name: human trafficking. As in the past, slaves come from all over the world. Not all are seized from their homes by force or captured as the result of war. Traffickers coerce people into physical work of various kinds, which is known as labor trafficking. Or victims may be forced into prostitution and other areas of the sex trade. This kind of human trafficking is called sex trafficking.

Some trafficked individuals are trapped in bondage to pay off a debt. Others agree to take jobs based on false promises. When they are under the control of their new bosses—often far from family, home, and any support systems they might turn to for help—they realize that they have been deceived. At other times, people *are* taken against their will. They may be kidnapped or their poverty-stricken families might sell them into slavery.

Baby trafficking is big business in China. This woman was recently charged with involvement in baby trafficking over the course of several years.

Like their victims, traffickers come from all over the world and from a variety of circumstances. Some trafficking is carried out by organized crime networks comprised of hundreds of people working together in a highly coordinated group, often called a trafficking ring. But a lot of trafficking is done on a much smaller scale, by single traffickers or by small groups in a neighborhood, a town, or a region.

Traffickers use a variety of methods to keep their victims in fear and bondage. People who have been trafficked are often isolated and may be in a country where they don't know the language. Traffickers often deprive victims of their passports and other vital documents, making travel difficult or impossible. Many traffickers abuse their captives physically, verbally, and sexually. When they suspect that a trafficked person might try to escape, they may also threaten to hurt that person's family.

Sometimes traffickers know their victims, who may be neighbors, casual acquaintances, or even relatives or friends. This personal connection can make it easier for traffickers to intimidate their victims and more difficult for captives to escape.

BIG BUSINESS

Human trafficking is a $30- to $45-billion industry, one of the most profitable businesses in the world. These profits rival those of the illegal sale and trade of drugs and weapons. Some experts point to human trafficking as the fastest growing of these underground industries.

The growth of and profits from human trafficking are related to fierce competition in the global economy, where a company or an industry's

FACTS AND FIGURES

Statistics about trafficking vary widely because much human trafficking goes unreported. Sources including the United Nations and the US State Department provide the following estimates:

- Children make up about 27 percent of human trafficking victims around the world. Two of every three trafficked children are girls.
- Women make up 55 to 60 percent of those who are trafficked.
- About 50 to 60 percent of traffickers are men.
- An estimated 46 percent of people who are trafficked know the traffickers who recruited them.
- Identified victims of trafficking come from more than 130 different countries and live and work in more than 115 countries.
- Experts believe that between 500,000 and 800,000 people are trafficked across international borders annually, with an estimated 17,000 or more trafficked into the United States each year. At any given time, up to 20 to 27 million people around the world are believed to be victims of some form of human trafficking.

access to cheap labor is key to gaining an economic advantage over competitors. When cheap labor is difficult to obtain, some people and industries are willing to turn to human trafficking.

As the world's economies grow increasingly interdependent, the opportunity gap between nations and peoples grows wider. Residents of poor countries are often desperate, and they are willing to migrate to find work. They are prepared to endure separation from their families, harsh working conditions, and uncertain futures, all of which put them at risk of exploitation by traffickers. Individual traffickers, on the other hand, are willing to risk their own capture and imprisonment to make a living—sometimes a very profitable one, even in poor countries.

WHO IS AT RISK?

Vulnerable and oppressed populations the world over are most at risk of exploitation by traffickers. Poverty is one of the main reasons that people fall victim to trafficking—or, in some cases, become traffickers themselves.

Women and children are most at risk for becoming victims of human trafficking. These women, at work in a stone quarry in northern India, are victims of a form of labor trafficking called debt bondage, in which workers toil for low wages to pay off exorbitant fees charged by the traffickers. The workers are rarely able to pay off their debts.

Gender and age are other major factors. Most people who are trafficked are women and children—especially girls and orphans—and most traffickers are men. Lack of education is another piece of the trafficking puzzle, and it often exists side by side with poverty. In addition, ethnic minorities are frequently the victims of trafficking.

Natural disasters and other unexpected calamities can also impact the patterns of human trafficking. When a catastrophe such as an earthquake, a hurricane, or a tsunami strikes a country, it can disrupt everything from the economy to social systems. If that country's citizens are already struggling, the impact of the disaster is even more extreme and people become more vulnerable to the lure of trafficking.

Health problems are yet another factor affecting human trafficking. The ravages of disease—from cholera to malaria to human immunodeficiency virus/acquired immunodeficiency syndrome (HIV/AIDS)—leave behind orphans, single parents, and others struggling to survive. They, as well as people living with disabilities, may be especially vulnerable to exploitation.

In addition, people who live in countries that have been disrupted by violent conflict or that have unstable or corrupt governments are at a higher risk for being trafficked. The African nation of Sudan, for example, has a history rife with rebellion, civil war, and ethnic and religious tensions. At different times in Sudan's history, Arab Sudanese have raided villages, kidnapped black Sudanese—many of them children—and enslaved them as household servants, field workers, and animal tenders.

Abeeda

Abuk Bak was one of these enslaved Sudanese children. She was kidnapped from her village, separated from her family, and sold in a town market to a man named Ahmed Adam. She spent the next ten years working for him and his family. She received little to eat and was beaten for even the smallest mistakes. The family never called her by her name. They called her only *abeeda,* an Arabic term meaning "black slave."

Former First Lady Eleanor Roosevelt of the United States holds a printed copy of the United Nations' Universal Declaration of Human Rights in 1948. The First Lady was a human rights activist and chaired the committee that drafted the declaration.

"EQUAL AND INALIENABLE RIGHTS"

The United Nations' Universal Declaration of Human Rights was ratified by the United Nations in 1948. The UN crafted the declaration in light of the atrocities committed during World War II (1939–1945), and it defines a list of rights to which all people around the globe are entitled.

Human trafficking violates many of the articles of this declaration. They include the following:

Article 1: All human beings are born free and equal in dignity and rights.

Article 4: No one shall be held in slavery or servitude; slavery and the slave trade shall be prohibited in all their forms.

Article 5: No one shall be subjected to torture or to cruel, inhuman or degrading treatment or punishment.

Abuk remembers, "On my second day there, Ahmed Adam sent me out alone with the goats. It didn't matter to him that I was only twelve years old, that I had no idea where I was, or that I had never done this kind of work before. It would now be my job to take care of about twenty animals and to see that every one of them returned home. . . . [One day when] Ahmed Adam counted and realized that I had lost a goat, he beat me severely with a stick and then sent me out into the night to search for the missing goat."

Abuk eventually ran away and reclaimed her freedom. Experts believe that raids like the one in which she was taken have become less common in Sudan.

However, neighboring Eritrea has been in upheaval for more than two decades. Many thousands of Eritreans have fled across the border into eastern Sudan, where they live in camps for refugees. Since about 2009, many residents of these camps have disappeared. Groups such as Amnesty International believe that refugees are being kidnapped and trafficked into Egypt, where they may be sold into bonded labor, forced into marriage, exploited for sex, or held for ransom. While in Egypt, many of these trafficked Eritreans are beaten, raped, and tortured.

The Paolettis

The Paoletti family moved to the United States from Mexico City. Many members of the family were deaf. They knew that in Mexico, some deaf people sold small items on the streets, earning just a few pesos per sale. They believed that the same idea could be successful—and more profitable—in the United

A sign-language interpreter speaks with a group of fifty-seven Mexican immigrants in New York City. The immigrants, all of whom are deaf, were recruited to be part of the Paoletti trafficking ring of peddlers, who sold trinkets on the streets of the city in the late 1990s.

States. So they set up a ring of trafficked labor in the United States made up of deaf Mexican men and women. They convinced their recruits that the move would improve their lives. As the sister of one recruited man recalled, "[My brother] said that by working less than he was in Mexico, he'd be able to buy a car . . . that's how [the Paolettis] won his heart."

The family's recruits immigrated to the United States—usually illegally. Most did not speak English, so they were largely dependent on

VOICES OF THE TRAFFICKERS: THE PAOLETTIS

The Paolettis were, in many ways, a lot like their victims. They had grown up in Mexico, and although they had not been poor, they hoped for more. They studied hard and worked hard. And most were deaf.

Jose Paoletti Moreda was one of the ringleaders of the family's operation. He described his treatment of the trafficked immigrants: "I told them to go to work and if they didn't bring back money, I would hurt them." At trial, Adriana Paoletti Lemus apologized for her actions and begged for the court's mercy. "I have two children, and I miss them terribly," she said.

What drove the Paolettis to do what they did? Is it possible that the family initially believed they were helping these men and women by bringing them to the United States? Or was profit their only motivation? Back in Mexico, people had mixed views of the family. Griselda Espinosa Chavez, a teacher of deaf children in Mexico, knew and praised many of the Paolettis. "These are fine people with great hearts," she said. "They were fighting to get ahead. They loved money and wanted a higher status."

Others had a very different point of view. "Don Paoletti was very nice, but I never trusted him," Pilar Muniz Rodriguez—the mother of one of the Paolettis' recruits—recalled. "I knew there was something wrong about the way he talked to me."

the Paolettis to help them make their way. The Paolettis put their recruits to work in US cities such as Los Angeles, California; Chicago, Illinois; and Miami, Florida.

The family set up their largest operation in New York City. They forced the men and women they had trafficked to peddle key chains and other trinkets on the subways or on street corners for one dollar apiece. At day's end, they demanded that the immigrant workers hand over whatever they had earned, sometimes physically searching their clothes and bodies for the money. If the workers hadn't brought in enough money, the family often beat them. The Paolettis also sexually assaulted some of the recruits.

In 1997, after four of the trafficked men went to the police, police raided two apartments in New York City where the Paolettis' victims lived. They discovered more than fifty of the deaf Mexican immigrants living in the small, crowded apartments. Law enforcement officials broke up the trafficking ring, and several members of the Paoletti family went to jail. Eduardo, one of the Paoletti recruits, described his ordeal with the help of a sign language interpreter. "We got almost nothing to eat," he said. "We had to sell every day, from six in the morning until seven at night. The boss had a very big house, but he did not give us anything."

Victims of labor trafficking may work behind the scenes as dishwashers and cooks. Many work in full view as servers in restaurants or in the agricultural and construction industries.

No one cares whether we die. . . . Our lives have no value.

—*a Nepalese man trafficked to Kuwait as a laborer, 2011*

Long days. Little or no pay. Abusive bosses. Isolation. Constant fear.

These are the facts of daily life for many victims of labor trafficking. According to the United Nations, the International Labour Organization (ILO), and other organizations that monitor trafficking, labor trafficking makes up between 35 and 65 percent of all human trafficking—equaling anywhere from 7 to 17.5 million people. Those who are forced to work are trafficked into many different types of jobs, from restaurant cooks and servers to street vendors, farmhands, and construction workers.

THE LAND OF THE FREE

In pursuit of better lives, thousands of immigrants come to the United States every year. Some arrive legally, while others enter the country illegally, without proper documentation. Many immigrants do find better lives in the United States. But for others, dishonest companies and labor recruiters take advantage of vulnerable workers, especially those who have immigrated illegally.

In a major labor trafficking case in 2010, the Federal Bureau of Investigation (FBI) formally charged several top executives of a US-based company called Global Horizons Manpower, Inc., with trafficking forced laborers. The case had come to the attention of authorities in 2003, when a trafficked laborer escaped and went public with his story. It was the largest human trafficking case in US history—but the case never went to court. The US government's lawyers dropped the case when a similar case was also dropped, casting doubt on whether the government would be able to prove aspects of the charges beyond a reasonable doubt.

The Global Horizons case involved the recruitment of hundreds of laborers to the United States from Thailand. Global Horizons told the men they would have well-paying jobs working on US farms. Part of this promise was true: the Thai laborers *did* go to work on farms. Most ended up in Hawaii, picking fruits, vegetables, and coffee beans. According to former workers, however, the good wages never materialized. The men say that they received very low pay—or none at all. In fact, the laborers actually paid fees of up to $21,000 to Global Horizons for placing them in agricultural jobs. These sums were huge for the Thai men, many of whom earned only about $1,000 per year in their home country. Many workers said that while they worked for Global Horizons, they lived in squalid conditions, sometimes sharing tiny quarters with many other men and without access to indoor plumbing.

Global Horizons had also told the workers they would receive the necessary work visas to stay in the United States legally while they were employed. But ex-workers say that Global Horizons only arranged temporary visas. When these permits expired after a few weeks, the men were unsure of what their rights were in a country where they had suddenly become illegal immigrants and did not speak the language well. Workers also say that Global Horizons took away their passports. With no form of identification, the Thai laborers were afraid to go to the police for fear they would be jailed or deported. Yet despite the many obstacles, in

VOICES OF THE VICTIMS

After the Global Horizons case was dropped, some of the workers sent a letter to the US attorney general, Eric Holder. In this letter, they expressed what they had been through and how disappointed they were.

We are the Thai farm workers who were victims of labor trafficking in the Global Horizons Manpower Case. It was not easy for us to come here. We have had to incur enormous debts and submit ourselves to tremendous hardship and exploitation, but we came because we could scarcely provide for our families with the meager resources we have at home. We have left behind our families with the hope that we would receive a just wage for our labor. Instead, we were forced into a terrible situation that none of us had expected. . . . [We] believed that we could find justice in this country. . . . We are sorry that this case has come to an abrupt end without ever being tried. We are especially sorry because we know what we have undergone and what we are still enduring today because of Global and nothing is ever going to change that fact.

2003 one of the Thai workers escaped and told his story and that of his fellow laborers, eventually gaining them their freedom.

"I FELT LIKE I WAS GOING TO JAIL"

In a similar case, South Korean businessman Kil Soo Lee owned and operated a garment factory called Daewoosa in the Pacific island territory of American Samoa. To staff his factory, which made clothes for US stores such as Target and J. C. Penney, Lee recruited hundreds of seamstresses and other garment workers from Vietnam and China. Lee charged each of these workers an initial fee of up to $6,000, promising them wages that were much higher than they could earn in their homelands. He also demanded that they agree to three-year work contracts. If a worker quit before the period was over, Lee would impose a penalty of thousands of dollars.

Lee's employees soon found that their wages were much lower than promised, if they were paid at all. Meanwhile, Lee monitored and controlled nearly every aspect of the workers' lives. He decided what and how much the workers ate. He then charged them for the food, even though most workers became malnourished from the meager amounts they received. Lee also charged his employees rent to live in filthy, crowded dorms, some of which did not have running water. The factory and living quarters were surrounded by fences and razor wire, and security guards patrolled the grounds. One former worker said, "I felt like I was going to jail." Workers were routinely threatened and beaten, and many female laborers were sexually assaulted. Lee reportedly told guards to beat laborers who worked too slowly, tried to escape, or complained about conditions.

Finally, one of the Daewoosa workers was able to get a note to the outside world, asking for help. The FBI looked into the matter, and Lee was arrested in 2001. (The company stopped operating the same year.) Lee was convicted of crimes including extortion (using force or threats to obtain money, services, or property from a person) and was sentenced to forty years in prison.

BEHIND CLOSED DOORS

Forced domestic servitude (also called involuntary domestic servitude) is a specific type of labor trafficking. Trafficked domestic servants work as maids, cooks, housekeepers, and nannies for individual people, couples, or families. They are typically women and are paid very little, if anything.

This type of forced labor can be especially hard for governments to monitor and control because it is largely hidden from view. Domestic servants usually live in the homes of the people they work for. Many of the workers initially accept their jobs voluntarily but are then threatened, forbidden to leave, or commanded to not speak to anyone outside the home.

VOICES OF THE VICTIMS: MARTINA

Martina Okeke came to the United States from Nigeria in 1988. She was a widow with two children. Martina arrived in Staten Island, New York, believing that she would earn $300 a month working for a Nigerian American couple there. The couple also told her that they would help pay for her children to go to school back in Nigeria. In return, Martina had to spend long days cleaning house, caring for the couple's children, and cooking for the family.

Martina did the work—but the couple never paid her the money she had been promised. In fact, she says that she worked for twelve years without ever being paid at all. She finally left the family in 2000, with the help and support of friends she'd made outside the home. However, Martina remained afraid to tell the police about what she had gone through. "I did not want to have a bad name," she said. "That somebody took me from Nigeria to America and I made trouble for them. I know my people. They would say I went to America to make trouble. That would not be good for me."

Martina still lives in New York and works caring for children. But she is free, and she is paid for her work.

A wealthy Egyptian couple brought this young woman from a poor village in northern Egypt to work in their home in California when she was only ten years old. For almost ten years, she worked for the family for up to twenty hours each day, ironing clothes, mopping elegant marble floors, and dusting the family's expensive crystal. She earned only forty-five dollars a month for her labor. Trafficking of young people for domestic labor is common in Africa as well as the United States.

Amina, a woman who went from Bangladesh to Lebanon to work as a maid, was one of these servants. She felt imprisoned in her situation, where she was physically and sexually abused, deprived of adequate food, and forbidden to step foot outside her employer's home for three months. As she later said, "[Kept] in solitary confinement in a room, I had no idea what Lebanon looked like."

In other cases, workers may be allowed to come and go but are threatened and intimidated into keeping their situations secret. This scenario makes it nearly impossible for these trafficked workers to get help, especially if they do not speak the local language and do not have proper work visas or other legally required documents. In addition, the private nature of domestic servitude tends to conceal the abuse—physical and sexual—that many trafficked domestic servants suffer behind the doors of the family home.

A HIGH PRICE TO PAY

Around the world, debt bondage, or bonded labor, is one of the most common forms of labor trafficking. Bonded laborers are forced to work to pay off debts to traffickers. Often a worker's entire family will work together. In some cases, the debt is a fee that the workers have paid to get the job, for transportation to the job site, for rent on a plot of land to farm, or for other services or goods. Other times, the person may be forced to work to pay off the debt of a relative who was unable or unwilling to pay off an earlier debt or who died before paying off a debt.

Requiring someone to pay off a contractual debt is not an illegal or unusual practice. Bonded labor, on the other hand, is a form of trafficking because bosses use a variety of methods to exploit their workers, making the debts virtually impossible to repay.

Sometimes trafficked workers who are in debt bondage believe that they know approximately how long it will take them to pay back the amount they owe. But in most cases, the debt never seems to shrink. It may even grow, even as the laborer works long hours, usually without any days off. As Anti-Slavery International puts it, "The value of [the trafficked laborer's] work becomes invariably greater than the original sum of money borrowed."

One reason for this is that the bonded worker is only paid a very small amount. Additionally, many employers take money out of the laborers' wages every week or every month. These deductions are frequently unfair and may even be charged for made-up expenses. For example, a maid may be falsely accused of breaking a vase and then forced to pay for it. Or a construction worker may be charged a hugely inflated amount for the tools and materials he needs to do his job. Some bonded workers live in housing rented out by their bosses. In all of these cases, most of the money that the workers do earn goes right back to the people who are exploiting them for their labor.

As in many other cases of labor trafficking, the person holding workers in debt bondage often forces them to labor under very harsh conditions.

Bosses and traffickers may also threaten the workers or their families with violence if they attempt to flee.

"Nobody leaves his own family because they want to; they are forced by hunger and poverty."

—a Romanian man who was trafficked to Hungary to work in construction, 2005

THE CYCLE OF SLAVERY

The ILO estimates that debt bondage enslaves more than twelve million people. Although the practice takes place all over the world, it is especially common in Asia and Latin America. Anti-Slavery International estimates that India alone is home to at least two million and perhaps as many as ten million bonded laborers. Other nations with high numbers of debt-bonded laborers include Pakistan, Paraguay, and Peru.

In many of these countries, historical traditions play a role in continuing the practice. In India, for example, the long-standing caste system has divided people into different categories, or classes. The lowest caste is the Dalits, sometimes known as the "Untouchables." A large proportion of the bonded workers in India—especially in rural areas— are members of this Dalit caste. Many work on farms and are paid not with money but with tiny portions of food, such as wheat or rice, to feed themselves and their families.

Baldev, a low-caste farmworker in northern India, describes his situation. "My family's worked for the same master for a long time. . . . I inherited my father's debt, so I always knew I'd be a *halvaha* [plowman]." Baldev's wages, like those of many bonded workers, are not enough to pay for fertilizer and irrigation for his fields, medicine for his family, and other necessities. And while he can sell crops that he grows on a small plot of land—if he has enough left over after feeding his family—the money he earns this way doesn't add up to much. So to cover his expenses, Baldev borrows money from his "master." This borrowed money comes with a high interest rate, increasing Baldev's debt bit by bit, again and again. Some laborers like Baldev may work for decades trying to pay off a debt that starts out as small as twenty-five dollars.

This system is deeply ingrained in India. As one landlord states, "Of course I have bonded laborers: I'm a landlord. I keep them and their families and they work for me."

Other bonded laborers in India make a wide variety of products including rugs, jewelry, and soccer balls. An estimated forty-five thousand Indian children labor in factories that manufacture fireworks. Some are as young as four years old. They work long days handling dangerous, flammable chemicals to pay back debts that their families owe to traffickers. Recruiters for the factories hire the children and give their families an advance on the wages their sons and daughters will earn. The children then work to pay off this loan.

India's neighbor Pakistan is also home to bonded laborers—an estimated three million or more. As in India, many of them are farmers. Other Pakistani bonded laborers are brick makers. Often whole families

The production of almost all the world's soccer balls involves child labor and debt bondage. In this photo, a young worker stitches a soccer ball at a factory in Jalandhar, India.

toil together, digging clay, shaping bricks, or firing the bricks in redhot kilns. The workday begins before dawn and may last through the hottest part of the day (with temperatures that regularly exceed 100°F, or 38°C) and into the evening. Owners of the brick kilns sometimes seize children of bonded laborers. They hold them as a way to prevent the family from trying to escape. These traffickers may also force laborers' children to work as servants in their homes.

A BITTER CROP

In West Africa, one of the industries most closely associated with slavery is cocoa production. The Ivory Coast exports more cocoa than any other

MINING FOR MISERY

The mining of diamonds, other gemstones, and precious metals is an industry with a history of forced labor. Some diamonds are known as "blood diamonds" or "conflict diamonds." These gems are typically mined in nations that are at war or are embroiled in internal conflict. The profits made from selling the diamonds are then used to fund further fighting—whether on behalf of an insurgency, an army, or a warlord. These blood diamonds are often—but not always—mined by trafficked laborers.

Even gems that are not blood diamonds are frequently the products of slave labor. In countries including Angola, Sierra Leone, and Zimbabwe, miners are sometimes trapped in debt bondage. In other cases, people—both adults and children—have been kidnapped or otherwise forced to work in mines. In Zimbabwe, for example, the army took control of diamond mines in 2008 and demanded that local men, women, and children do the difficult and often dangerous work of mining. Those who resisted—or who went to work but refused to give the soldiers their earnings—were beaten, raped, tortured, or even killed. Forced labor also fuels gold mining operations in countries including Burkina Faso, North Korea, and Peru, jade mining in Burma, and silver mining in Bolivia.

Labor exploitation, particularly of children, is common in the world's harvest of cacao (for the production of chocolate). When you buy chocolate, look for certification by Fairtrade International, Rainforest Alliance, or UTZ Certified. These groups are part of a global organization known as the ISEAL Alliance that works to ensure fair labor practices for workers in a range of industries, including cocoa production.

nation—about one-third of all the cocoa produced in the world, which then goes into a huge range of chocolate products. To keep up with demand, cocoa plantation owners in the Ivory Coast often turn to slave labor.

Some of these slaves are adults, but many more are children—an estimated half million. These children may be sold into the work by poor families. Others are kidnapped—often from neighboring countries such as Burkina Faso and Mali. While the average age of children on cocoa farms is between twelve and sixteen, some children are as young as seven. The work they do is difficult and dangerous. Cocoa farmers use machetes to hack open large cacao pods to reach the beans within. Many workers injure themselves. In addition, trafficked workers on plantations are often whipped or beaten for working too slowly or for trying to flee. They are usually not given enough food to eat, and they live in squalid housing where they are often locked in at night. Child workers are usually not allowed to go to school.

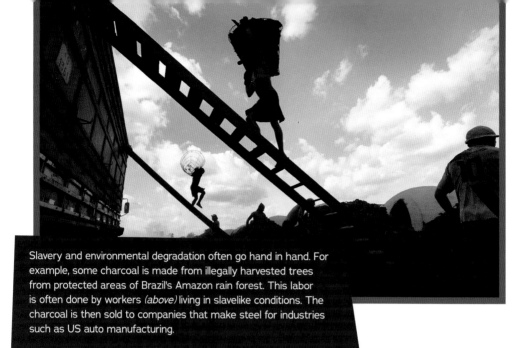

Slavery and environmental degradation often go hand in hand. For example, some charcoal is made from illegally harvested trees from protected areas of Brazil's Amazon rain forest. This labor is often done by workers *(above)* living in slavelike conditions. The charcoal is then sold to companies that make steel for industries such as US auto manufacturing.

"ALL MY LIFE I'VE BEEN HERE"

In Central and South America, indigenous peoples are at high risk of being trafficked. They are generally poor and rank low in the region's social order. In Paraguay, for instance, indigenous workers are held in debt bondage in numbers that are disproportionate to their share of the nation's population. While the country's indigenous peoples make up less than 2 percent of the total residents, the ILO estimates that 10 percent of indigenous Paraguayans are bonded laborers. Most of these laborers work on cattle ranches in the Gran Chaco, a rugged area comprising portions of several South American nations. The Chaco region extends into Bolivia, where many indigenous Guarani people work as bonded laborers in jobs such as cattle ranching, gathering chestnuts, and other agricultural labor.

Teresa Barrio is one of the Guarani workers. A sixty-five-year-old grandmother, she has worked on the same Bolivian farm since childhood. "All my life I've been here and at the end of it, I have nothing and have nowhere else to go," she says.

In Peru the timber industry is a major employer of trafficked workers. These laborers do the difficult, dangerous, and environmentally damaging work of logging trees, often doing so illegally in Peru's rain forests. An estimated twenty thousand to thirty-three thousand workers are bonded into this labor. They usually live in rustic camps along with their families. They are paid little and are often charged for the tools they need to do their jobs. In some cases, armed guards patrol the camps and work sites. As in Paraguay and Bolivia, a high proportion of the bonded workers are members of the country's indigenous population. Some observers estimate that 75 percent of all indigenous Peruvians are held in debt bondage.

A BLOODY TRADE

A unique and very specific kind of trafficking deals not with people but with *parts* of people: organ trafficking. Selling human organs is against the law in most countries. But a black market has long existed, dealing illegally in vital organs such as kidneys, livers, and lungs, all of which are in short supply the world over. Some desperately ill people around the globe are willing to pay very high prices and engage in illegal transactions for the lifesaving organs.

Poverty drives some people to sell their own body organs. Each of these Pakistani men shows a scar from an operation to remove a kidney. The men sold the organs for about $1,700 each to hospitals that then earned many thousands of dollars more from wealthy patients in need of kidney transplants.

Sometimes the people whose organs are removed choose to sell them voluntarily, even though it is illegal to do so. Most agree to this gruesome trade only because they are very poor. As in many cases of human trafficking, the people who have given up their organs are often paid less than they were promised—or nothing at all. In other cases, organ "donors" are threatened or held against their will.

After an illegal transplant operation, the person who has sold his or her organ does not always get good medical care and may suffer from infections or other complications. In some cases, traffickers have hidden or destroyed donor patients' medical records. They do this to make it more difficult for law enforcement officials to find and prosecute the responsible parties. However, the missing records also make it more challenging for the organ donors to get follow-up care after their operations.

Organ trafficking operations have been revealed in countries including Bangladesh, Ukraine, Kosovo, Brazil, and the Philippines. Traffickers also operate from the United States. In 2009 the FBI arrested a Brooklyn, New York, man who was buying organs in Israel for about $10,000 per organ, then selling them to Americans for more than fifteen times that amount.

Police in India have broken up numerous trafficking rings involving doctors, nurses, and paramedics as well as people untrained in medicine. One of the largest operations was uncovered in 2008, when authorities identified a group headed by two brothers that they believe carried out up to five hundred illegal kidney transplants over an estimated period of six or seven years. While some of the poor and uneducated workers and farmers who sold their organs did so willingly, others were threatened at gunpoint and forced to undergo the surgeries. Of the donors who did actually receive money in return for their kidneys, most were paid only a tiny fraction of what the traffickers later earned on the trade. Indian police believe that donors were paid about $1,000 or less per organ, while the traffickers sold the organs for up to $37,500 each.

China is another country with a thriving black market in human organs. In 2012 Chinese authorities arrested 137 people suspected of organ trafficking. Hu Jie was one of the many people caught up in this illegal trade. He decided to sell a kidney to pay off debts. But at the last minute, he got nervous and unsure. Before he could leave, Hu was tied to an operating table in "a dark room, cold and shabby." Hu remembers, "The nurse inserted a huge needle into my body, and I soon passed out."

Organ trafficking is also on the rise in eastern Europe. The global economic downturn that began in about 2007 left many people looking for any way to support their families. Pavel Mircov, a father of two in Serbia, made the decision to sell one of his organs. He explained, "When you need to put food on the table, selling a kidney doesn't seem like much of a sacrifice."

Chapter 3

SEX SELLS

Young girls around the globe are exploited through sex trafficking and prostitution. This teen prostitute in Bangladesh sees fifteen to twenty customers each day. She lives in a prisonlike brothel, where she earns less than ten dollars a day. To gain weight and appear healthier to her clients, she takes a steroid called Oradexon, a common practice in Bangladeshi brothels. The drug is highly addictive and can lead to diabetes, high blood pressure, and kidney failure.

We are like ghosts. We are literally shadows on the highway.

—Frida, a Nigerian woman forced into prostitution in Italy, 2013

Some experts believe that sex trafficking, mostly in the form of forced prostitution, accounts for more than 70 percent of all trafficking, or as many as 19 million people. Others maintain that sex trafficking actually comprises a relatively small portion of trafficking overall but appears in the news much more often. Similarly, statistics vary widely regarding how much money sex trafficking generates, with estimates ranging anywhere from $5 billion a year globally to more than $15 billion a year in Latin America alone.

Bodies for Sale: A Day in the Lives of Trafficked Sex Workers

Crowded into rundown apartments and cramped, filthy trailers, the girls and the women had sex with up to thirty "customers" a day. At all times, the girls and the women were closely guarded. Many were beaten and raped by brothel guards and the trafficking bosses. On the rare occasions the captives were allowed to call home, guards listened in and prevented them from telling their families about the terrifying situation.

These were the daily lives of girls and women trafficked by the Cadena-Sosa family. The Cadena-Sosa family immigrated to Florida from Mexico. On return visits, they promised local Mexican women and girls jobs as nannies and waitresses. Because most who accepted the offers did not have visas to work in the United States, they agreed to be smuggled into the country illegally. They had to pay a fee for this service, racking up large debts. And when the girls and the women arrived in Florida, the Cadena-Sosas forced them to work as prostitutes. The family took half the women's meager earnings. In the end, the women made only about three dollars per customer.

But the women still needed money to pay for food, for phone calls home, and for the skimpy lingerie the Cadena-Sosas forced them to wear on the job. Some of the women became pregnant and were forced to have abortions. For all of these expenses, they had to borrow money—from the Cadena-Sosas. "My debt continued to grow," says a victim named Rosa. "There seemed to be no end to my nightmare."

Eventually, some victims escaped and alerted authorities. The FBI raided the brothels, arresting many members of the family. Some of the Cadena-Sosas were convicted of their crimes, but others still remain at large.

Sex trafficking primarily affects women and girls, but men and boys are also trafficked into sex work. In countries including Afghanistan and Sri Lanka, boys are sold into forced prostitution with male clients, while Brazilian men have been discovered as sex trafficking victims in Spain. Overall, men and boys make up about 2 percent of the victims of sex trafficking.

Victims are often held at brothels and forced to have sex with many clients every day. Some women are made to work as strippers, often in sex clubs that also have prostitutes offering sex for sale. A small number of trafficking victims are forced to perform in pornographic films.

NIGHT BARS

The Balkan region of eastern Europe is a major source of women who are trafficked to other parts of the continent as sex workers. Bosnia, Serbia, and other Balkan countries have a relatively recent history of war and political instability, and poverty is widespread. Some women—desperate for jobs to support themselves or their families—answer newspaper classifieds, online posts, or other advertisements for restaurant servers, house cleaners, or nannies. When these women respond to the ads, many find that they have been tricked into working as prostitutes. By the time they fully realize what has happened, it is often too late to get away safely.

Sex trafficking and prostitution are common in poverty-stricken, war-torn regions of the world or in areas that have a recent history of bloody conflict. Many women and girls in the nations of former Yugoslavia, for example, are vulnerable to sex traffickers. Sex workers are at high risk of violence at the hands of their traffickers, pimps, and clients.

Many of these trafficked women work in night bars, or nightclubs that double as brothels. In some cases, the women are sold at auctions, which may take place at brothels (legal and illegal), the back rooms of bars, or apartments that traffickers have rented to hold their victims. Potential buyers from all over Europe view the women, sometimes forcing them to strip and to dance or walk around to be viewed from every angle. One former victim, a Moldavian girl named Stefa, was held at a Serbian apartment building with dozens of other trafficked girls and women. Stefa was sixteen at the time. She recalled, "At all hours, these men arrived and we would have to take off our clothes and stand in front of them. They wanted to see what we looked like naked. They touched us and examined us like we were cattle. Sometimes they took us to a room to see how we performed sexually."

Once they have been bought and sold, trafficking victims may stay in their home country or be moved to other nations to be part of the sex trade there. At the brothels, clubs, and auctions, guards—usually armed—prevent the women from escaping by beating, torturing, and raping them. These guards may also issue threats against the women's families, including threatening to traffic their younger sisters or to kill their parents or children.

Other Balkan women, accepting what they think are legitimate jobs in nearby Italy, do not find what they are hoping for. Some never end up in Italy at all but instead are trafficked by recruiters into Turkey or to other nations where they are sold into sexual slavery. Others do make it to Italy but are then forced into sex work there. Street prostitution is legal in Italy, but brothels are not. For that reason, many brothel owners in Italy disguise their businesses as strip clubs, which are legal.

Italy is a relatively short journey from northern Africa, and many women are trafficked between Africa and Italy. Most come from Nigeria. Like so many others, Gloria believed that she would find more opportunities by leaving behind the poverty she knew at home in Nigeria. "I dreamt about going to school, learning a trade, and getting married.

Nothing complicated," she explains. Instead, Gloria ended up working as a prostitute in Italy—one of an estimated ten thousand or more Nigerian prostitutes there. Many of these women are working against their will and under the threat of violence. Nigerian gangs often operate in Italy with the cooperation of the Italian Mafia. By paying the Mafia to look the other way—and to use its power to bribe or threaten local law enforcement and other officials—Nigerian traffickers are able to continue this practice and make large amounts of money.

A NATIONAL SECRET

Sex trafficking occurs within the United States every day. As in other forms of trafficking, the people most at risk are poor, female, and young. Immigrants and others who are marginalized by factors such as limited English-language skills are also in greater danger. And while girls and women are the most common victims of sex trafficking, boys and transgender youth are also at risk. Other high-risk groups for sex trafficking in the United States include young people who have been sexually abused as children.

"A pimp . . . took me to someone's place and he said this guy . . . [is] interested in you. Then he started hitting me after I said no. I was so scared I just did it. After that I kept doing it because I was afraid to get hit."

—an American Indian woman from Minnesota who was trafficked into prostitution, 2011

American Indian women are at especially high risk of trafficking and exploitation. Across the United States, American Indians as a group face more discrimination, higher levels of poverty, lower levels of education, and other challenges compared to the general population. For American

Indian women, this vulnerability also places them in greater danger of being trafficked.

Trafficking victims forced into sex work within the United States may end up working on the streets, in illegal brothels (often disguised as massage parlors), in apartments rented by traffickers, at strip clubs, or at truck stops. Traffickers rely on violence, threats, and emotional manipulation to keep their victims enslaved.

VOICES OF THE VICTIMS: BRIANNA

Brianna was twelve years old. One night, after an upsetting argument with her mother, Brianna decided to get out of the house. She ran out onto the streets of New York City, ending up at the apartment of the brother of a friend. She later described the frightening moment when she discovered that he had no intention of letting her go home. "I tried to leave, and he said, 'you can't go; you're mine.'" The man locked Brianna in his apartment and forced her to work as a prostitute. He used websites to sell her for sex. He also beat her and threatened her regularly, though at other times, he treated her gently and acted affectionately toward her.

Brianna was so close to home that while looking out of her trafficker's window, she once saw her mother hanging "missing person" posters on the lampposts outside. Brianna was close enough to call out to her mother—but she didn't dare. "If you shout, I'll kill you," Brianna remembers her captor telling her. "If I tried to run, I thought he might kill me, or I'd be hurt." She adds, "And, if I went to the cops, I thought I'd be the one in trouble. I'd go to jail."

Brianna eventually escaped and found help as she recovered from her ordeal. But she still lives with the fear and worry that her past will endanger her ability to create a good life for herself. All the same, she is working toward graduating from high school and hopes to become a lawyer.

SEX TOURISM

In some countries, sex tourism is a lucrative and shadowy industry, offering sex for a fee to tourists who visit the nation specifically to have sex with prostitutes. Around the world, sex tourism is a multibillion-dollar business. In some destination countries, such as the Netherlands and Colombia, prostitution is legal. In others, the laws governing prostitution are lax or under-enforced. Other sex tourism destinations include Brazil, Cambodia, the Dominican Republic, Kenya, the Philippines, and Thailand. Most sex tourists are men, usually seeking sex with women or girls. However, in countries including Indonesia, Jordan, and Senegal, a growing segment of the industry caters to women seeking male prostitutes. In nations where sex tourism is common, prostitutes may work in bars, nightclubs, and brothels, or they may be on the streets, beaches, or other public spaces.

Many (though not all) workers in the sex tourism industry have been trafficked. They are often tricked, kidnapped, or forced into prostitution and held against their will with force, threats, and intimidation. In addition, victims are trafficked from other nations into countries with thriving sex tourism industries. For example, some of the dancers and prostitutes in Thailand's bars and brothels come from nearby Cambodia, Burma, or Laos. Like the Thai women in the industry, some of the immigrant women have been tricked or kidnapped. But they are especially isolated because they often cannot speak Thai. They are also usually in the country illegally. If they are arrested, they may have trouble defending themselves or explaining their situation.

HIGH-TECH TRAFFICKING

In the twenty-first century, traffickers use a range of communication tools, including social networking, to recruit unsuspecting women and girls into prostitution. For example, in Alexandria, Virginia, Justin Strom was the leader of a gang that recruited teenage girls for prostitution. Strom created Facebook accounts under false names and used them to send messages to targeted girls and young women. In his messages, he usually complimented them on their appearance and asked if they would be interested in earning some money. If the recipient of one of these messages wrote back, Strom or one of his fellow traffickers would try to set up a meeting with her. At the face-to-face meeting, she would learn what the men really intended. At that point, it was often too late to back out. Girls who said no were threatened, assaulted, and sometimes forced to take drugs that dulled their senses and made it more difficult for them to protest or resist.

Strom was eventually arrested and charged with the sex trafficking of a child and the transportation of minors. One young woman who testified against him described the psychological trauma she endured. She said, "I met Justin Strom at 16. . . . He's a con artist, a monster, a manipulator. The same day I met him, I found myself, or lost myself, in the arms of thugs and hustlers. . . . I was brainwashed into believing that having sex with men for money was normal, an everyday thing."

Faking romantic relationships is another tactic that some traffickers use online with the women and girls they are targeting. In this situation, a trafficker creates a connection with his target, usually via Facebook or other social media. Over time, the trafficker convinces his prey that he is her devoted boyfriend. Gradually, with the relationship usually moving from online to the real world, he gains the young woman's trust before eventually demanding that she engage in prostitution. The trafficker then functions as her pimp, the man who arranges transactions between prostitutes and clients and who takes most of the money. If she refuses, he may coerce her by insisting that she prove her love for him by doing as he asks, by convincing her that prostitution is safe and that he wouldn't ask her to do it otherwise, by threatening to leave her, or by threatening her with physical harm. By this time, the woman (or teenage girl) is often deeply involved emotionally and may also be dependent on the man for money, housing, and safety, making it very difficult for her to say no to him.

VOICES OF THE TRAFFICKERS: JUSTIN STROM

At the end of Justin Strom's sentencing hearing, Strom himself spoke up and professed regret for his crimes. He told the court, "I'm sorry for the things that I've done, and I'm sorry for my actions. And I want to say to the families and the victims and to my family that I'm sorry for all the pain that I caused them." Strom recalled a time when he realized that what he was doing was wrong and that he wanted to change. "I looked in the mirror and I could see what I became and that's not what I wanted to be. That's not the type of person I want to be as a role model to my sons. And I decided I wanted to change from then. And from that day forth, I didn't have anything to do with any prostitution or receive any money from it."

According to Strom's lawyer, Thomas Carter, Strom was a victim of what Carter called a "toxic moral culture." At the time of sentencing, Carter said, "He does not fit the profile of some big-time pimp. He was living in a foreclosed house, where the electricity had been turned off. . . . He had $2 in his wallet and he was bumming cigarettes. . . . He was living in a perpetual fog of drugs and sex. There was no glamour."

Strom closed his statement by asking the judge for leniency in his sentencing. He said, "I can't blame anybody but myself. And I don't want to blame it on drugs or alcohol, but it had a big part. And I just—I'm sorry for the pain that I put these people through, and . . . I deserve to be punished for that." But, he asked, "Give me a second chance to be—to be a husband to my wife and be a father to my kids because I think they deserve that. . . . I just ask that—you know, I ask God to forgive me. I ask for mercy. Your Honor, I just ask that you have mercy on me."

Craigslist is another website that has played a role in sex trafficking. Until 2010 it featured an "erotic" category intended for consenting adults looking for sexual partners. Traffickers began to use it to advertise girls and women for prostitution. The women who were lured into the sex trade were sold at a different Craigslist site in major cities such as Philadelphia, Pennsylvania; Dallas, Texas; Milwaukee, Wisconsin; and Washington, DC. To shed light on this practice, two women who had been trafficked through Craigslist took out a newspaper ad describing their experiences. One, who used the initials "M.C." to protect her identity, wrote, "I was first forced into prostitution when I was 11 years old by a 28-year-old man. I am not an exception. The man who trafficked me sold many girls my age." M.C. went on, "I am 17 now, and my childhood memories aren't of my family, going to middle school, or dancing at the prom. They are [of] making my own arrangements on Craigslist to be sold for sex, and answering as many ads as possible for fear of beatings."

Craigslist shut down the adult section of its website in 2010 after public outcry and legal investigations in several states brought attention to the practice. But traffickers still use Craigslist and other sites to entice victims into the sex trade by using code language or by simply lying about their intentions. It's not difficult for online traffickers to evade laws, and although major websites monitor for illegal activity, they can't always keep up with the volume of new accounts and daily posts.

"I WAS THEIR SLAVE"

Not all sex trafficking leads to prostitution. In the early 2000s, several men originally from Ukraine and Lithuania were operating a company in the United States called Beauty Search. On the surface, the company was a recruitment and management service for eastern European women who wanted jobs in the United States. Once the women arrived in the country, the Beauty Search owners forced them to work at strip clubs in Detroit, Michigan. They physically abused the women and threatened them with death. The women were told they were obligated to work in the clubs and to hand over their wages to pay off alleged debts for their travel costs into the United States. The traffickers also kept the women isolated—even forbidding them to make phone calls. They took away their passports and threatened to turn them into the authorities as illegal immigrants if they

Young men and boys are also victims of sex trafficking around the globe. These two young Polish sex workers wait for clients in Berlin, Germany.

resisted or tried to leave. "They forced me to work six days a week for twelve hours a day," said one of the women. "I was often yelled at for not making enough money or had a gun put to my face. . . . I was their slave."

Meanwhile, according to officials, the men running Beauty Search made more than $1 million in about one year. Eventually, after two women escaped and went to authorities, nine people were convicted for this trafficking operation.

HEALTH HAZARDS

Men and women who work in the sex industry—whether they have been trafficked or not—face serious risks to their health. Experts estimate that 60 to 75 percent of women in prostitution have been raped and that 70 to 95 percent have been beaten or otherwise abused. Male prostitutes face similar dangers. In addition, workers in forced prostitution are often not able to perform safe sex because pimps don't allow it or clients refuse to use protection. Many women become pregnant. For example, one study found that one-third of sex workers in Cambodia had had an unwanted pregnancy in the previous year. Trafficked sex workers who become pregnant often have abortions, either by choice or because their traffickers insist. These procedures are sometimes done illegally and may not be performed by qualified doctors, putting the women in danger of complications that can leave them unable to have children and that can even be fatal.

Sex workers are also at high risk of contracting sexually transmitted diseases, including HIV/AIDS. For instance, in Ghana, Uganda, and Kenya, an estimated one-third of new HIV infections are among female sex workers. In Argentina, male sex workers have an infection rate of about 23 percent. And in Nepal, women and girls trafficked into India as sex workers had an estimated 38 percent infection rate. Sex workers—both trafficked and not—may not receive treatment for these diseases right away. Often traffickers and pimps don't want to spend money on medicine. In other cases, victims aren't educated about what their symptoms mean or are afraid of punishment if they raise concerns. What's more, workers who do become sick are often "fired." While this may release the trafficked victims from bondage, it also leaves them alone, gravely ill, usually penniless and without health insurance, and often not knowing who they can turn to for help.

INVISIBLE SCARS

Victims of sex trafficking may have their ordeals literally etched into their skin. Some sex traffickers burn their captives with branding irons to show possession. Others tattoo the workers under their control with bar codes or other symbols.

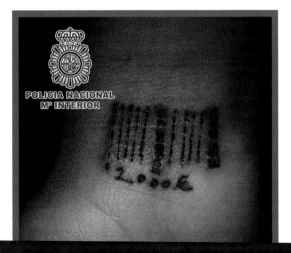

Sex traffickers sometimes tattoo their victims as a sign of ownership. This bar code tattoo on the wrist of a young Spanish woman includes "2,000 E," referring to a supposed debt (in euros) that her traffickers wanted to collect from her.

Former trafficking victims—especially those who have been forced into prostitution or other sex work—also suffer from unseen wounds. Many face ongoing mental and emotional issues from the trauma and abuse they have endured. Nightmares and anxiety can plague them for years. They may also suffer from post-traumatic stress disorder (PTSD), depression, and other emotional conditions related to their experiences. Many feel they have no future. Others lose their sense of personal safety as well as their trust in a meaningful life and a just world.

Some people who have been trafficked develop a psychological condition known as Stockholm syndrome, also called traumatic bonding. In this scenario, victims protect themselves mentally from the trauma of their experiences by developing feelings of affection for their captors and abusers.

In addition, some survivors of trafficking also face rejection and shame when friends and family shun them or refuse to talk about the taboo topics surrounding their experiences. Drug and alcohol abuse are also common among people who have been trafficked. One woman described trying to block out the pain she felt. "I would go to bed drunk because it was the only way I could fall asleep," she remembered.

Experts estimate that about one-third of the people trafficked globally are children. This young teen in Mexico is one of millions of child victims of sex traffickers.

At night I dream of what I have seen. I don't feel like a normal person.

—Sarah, a Ugandan girl who was captured by the Lord's Resistance Army when she was eight and became a wife before she was ten and a mother by the age of fourteen, 2007

Many victims of human trafficking are children—an estimated 27 percent of all trafficked persons, or about 5.4 million to 7.3 million victims. They may be sold into labor bondage or forced to engage in the sex industry. While children are caught up in all forms of human trafficking, many observers view child trafficking as a separate category of human trafficking. Children are uniquely vulnerable to exploitation and abuse, and certain forms of trafficking target children specifically.

SOLD FOR SEX

Estimates vary widely, but some experts think that about one million children are victims of sex trafficking each year. As many as ten million children and teens could be working in the sex trade globally. An estimated one hundred thousand or more of these victims are in the United States. Other nations with high numbers of children trafficked into sex work are Brazil, Cambodia, India, Malaysia, and Thailand. As in other forms of trafficking, girls are most often victimized, but boys are also at risk.

Children and teens are forced into sex work in a number of ways. In nations with a thriving sex tourism industry, such as Thailand, poor families desperate to gain a share of the profits may sell their children into the sex trade. In other cases, teens in impoverished rural areas are tricked by recruiters who promise them work in big cities. Other children are kidnapped and forced into prostitution.

In the United States, children and teens who run away from home are at especially grave risk of sexual exploitation. Experts state that one in three runaways will be lured into prostitution within forty-eight hours. On average, in the United States, kids enter the sex trade between the ages of twelve and fourteen.

VOICES OF THE VICTIMS: LIA

Lia works the streets as a cross-dressing prostitute in Recife, Brazil. At the age of fourteen, poverty had driven him into this work. "I hate it," he says. "I just do it because I need it." Lia's customers find him near the beaches and resort hotels of this oceanfront city. "They come in the car," explains Lia. They ask how much it is. I tell them, and . . . if they want me, they take me." Lia helps support himself and his mother with the money he earns—about twenty-five to fifty dollars per customer. He hopes someday to escape this life and become a nurse. He adds, "I would like to get married with someone I'm in love with. And quit doing what I do."

Sometimes pimps, madams (women who run brothels), and other traffickers lie to clients about the age of prostitutes, saying that they're older than they really are. But in other cases, clients specifically seek out very young girls or boys. In Cambodia, for example, many traffickers specialize in young girls. Some brothels have reportedly bought girls as young as three years old and consider twelve to be too old to work.

"I missed my family. I cried twice each night. I thought my parents must be thinking, 'Where is our son? Maybe he's dead.' The other children also cried and said, 'I want to go home to my family.' "

—a Burmese soldier, aged thirteen, 2002

CHILDREN AT WAR

Experts believe that since 2000, child soldiers have been engaged in conflicts in at least twenty-seven nations around the world. About half of these countries—including Liberia, Rwanda, Angola, and the Congo (both the Democratic Republic of the Congo and the Republic of the Congo)—are in Africa. Conflict in many nations in Asia (such as Afghanistan, India, Sri Lanka, and Nepal) and the Middle East (including Iran, Israel, and Yemen) also involve child soldiers.

The groups who traffic children into combat include official but unscrupulous government armies. They also include antigovernment rebel fighters and independent armed militias that may operate independently in war-torn areas. Children as young as seven years old come to be soldiers in a wide variety of ways. Some are poor, homeless, or orphaned and join armed groups voluntarily because they don't know how else to survive in poverty-stricken or war-torn regions. Many others are coerced through threats against them, their families, or their communities. Other child soldiers are kidnapped by soldiers in raids on villages or are abducted from their homes or from outdoor markets and other public spaces.

THE LORD'S RESISTANCE ARMY

The Lord's Resistance Army (LRA) is a violent, heavily armed rebel group in eastern Africa. According to UN estimates, the LRA has abducted more than sixty-six thousand children and teens since the 1980s to provide military manpower in conflicts in Sudan, Uganda, and the Congo. The LRA often raids villages and takes children captive, forcing them to join the army and to

A young soldier with the Lord's Resistance Army poses with his rifle. About 40 percent of the world's three hundred thousand child soldiers are involved in conflicts in Africa. Most are part of the LRA, a militia in which 90 percent of the soldiers are children. Founded by Joseph Kony, the LRA recruits boys from Uganda, the Central African Republic, the Democratic Republic of Congo, and Sudan to sustain violent conflict in the region.

kill—or be killed themselves. Sometimes these children must prove their courage to LRA soldiers by killing their own relatives. In other cases, they witness terrible violence against family members. One thirteen-year-old boy described his abduction and the brutal consequences:

> Early on when my brothers and I were captured, the LRA explained to us that all five brothers couldn't serve in the LRA because we would not perform well. So they tied up my two younger brothers and invited us to watch. Then they beat them with sticks until [they] died. They told us it would give us strength to fight. My youngest brother was nine years old.

Not all children abducted by militias are forced to fight. Some serve as spies. Others work as servants for the soldiers, doing cooking and housekeeping. Young girls are sometimes forced to become soldiers' wives, and both boys and girls may be sexually abused by the fighters who hold them captive. Sarah, a Ugandan girl, was captured by the LRA when she was eight and became a "wife" before she had reached her tenth birthday. She was a mother at the age of fourteen. She also had to fight and says she killed thirty people after being taken by the LRA.

FRACTURED FAMILIES

Another form of child exploitation is the trafficking of babies and children for adoption. Some nations—such as the United States, Italy, Spain, and Canada—have a high rate of international adoption. Because the number of healthy, adoptable infants does not meet global demand, traffickers around the world have responded by using illegal and dishonest methods to obtain babies.

China is one country with a high rate of adoption trafficking. Most of the trafficked children are sold into international adoption, but others are sold to Chinese families who want sons. China has a national policy allowing most families—especially the poor—to have only one child. (The policy was modified in 2013 to allow for some exceptions.) Because most Chinese couples want male heirs, they may sell, abandon, or kill daughters.

Some of these children—especially daughters—are sold by their parents. In other cases, they may be kidnapped when parents, siblings, or babysitters let down their guard, even momentarily. Peng Gaofeng, whose four-year-old son was kidnapped in the family's hometown of Shenzhen, China, recalls, "I turned away for a minute, and when I called out for him he was gone." Three years later, the boy and his family were reunited, but such stories rarely end on a happy note.

Traffickers in China also buy babies from corrupt doctors and other hospital staff, sometimes for as little as twelve dollars per child. For

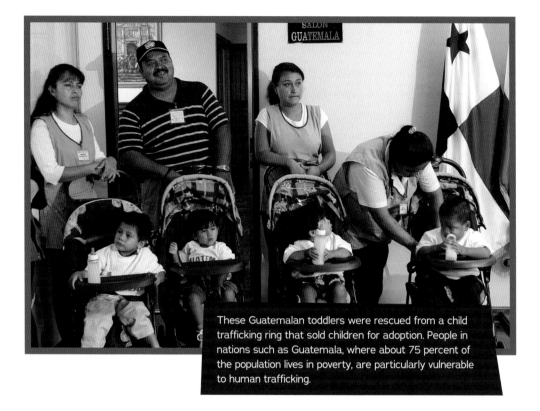

These Guatemalan toddlers were rescued from a child trafficking ring that sold children for adoption. People in nations such as Guatemala, where about 75 percent of the population lives in poverty, are particularly vulnerable to human trafficking.

example, obstetrician Zhang Shuxia is believed to have kidnapped and sold at least twenty-five infants. In most cases, she told new parents that their babies had died, that they were too ill to survive, or that they had severe handicaps and would need lifelong care. Zhang then sold these infants to orphanages. In turn, the orphanages sell the children to international adoption agencies. With high demand, traffickers can earn hundreds or even thousands of dollars per child. Some corrupt officials in the Chinese government also participate in this trade—for a cut of the profits. These government employees can arrange forged paperwork to convince foreign agencies and families that the adoption is legal.

In late 2012, police broke up a twelve-person trafficking ring in Russia that included midwives and hospital workers. The ring was revealed when one member tried to sell a newborn baby for $17,500 to an undercover police officer. Russian traffickers kidnap infants and sell them to well-off

Russians and to people from other countries. This form of trafficking is especially common in politically unstable and poor areas of the Russian Federation, such as Dagestan and Chechnya.

Other nations where adoption trafficking is common include Ethiopia, India, Vietnam, Nepal, and Guatemala. For years the practice seemed especially widespread in Guatemala. A Central American nation of about fifteen million people, Guatemala has lost a significant percentage of its children to adoption trafficking. Between 1998 and 2008, US families alone adopted nearly thirty thousand Guatemalan children—about 1 percent of the children born in Guatemala in that decade. Observers believe that many of these babies are not voluntarily put up for adoption by their parents. Some traffickers of infants disguise themselves as nurses and give new mothers sleeping pills and then take their babies before they wake up, telling them that the newborns have died. In other cases, traffickers may offer money to poor women in exchange for their babies, sometimes convincing them that their children will be better off with families in wealthier countries. Sophisticated traffickers then create fake files for each child, creating the illusion that the child is an orphan or has been willingly put up for adoption by the parents. In most cases, adoptive parents do not question such paperwork. In 2008 Guatemala officially ended international adoptions because of these accusations and suspicions. However, experts believe that adoption trafficking still takes place and has simply moved further underground.

"I was told she was an orphan. One year after she came home, and she could speak English well enough, she told me about her mommy and daddy and her brothers and her sisters."

—an American woman who unknowingly adopted a trafficked Cambodian girl, 2007

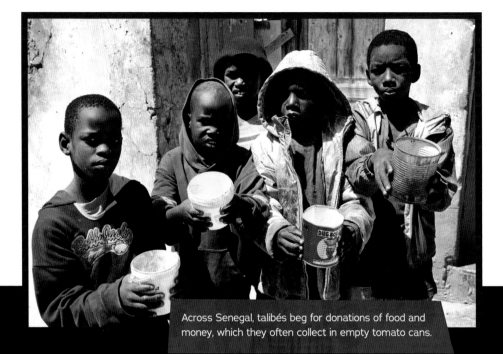

Across Senegal, talibés beg for donations of food and money, which they often collect in empty tomato cans.

"HE DIED, RIGHT NEXT TO ME": A DAY IN THE LIFE OF A TALIBÉ

In the West African nation of Senegal, many poor families struggle to support their children. In the hopes of giving them greater opportunities, some parents send their sons to live at Islamic schools, called *daaras*, in the cities. The schools' teachers are Islamic holy men called marabouts, and their students are known as *talibés*. The daaras have a long and proud tradition in the region. The schools have even educated some of the nation's leaders. Trusting in that tradition, families who send their sons to modern daaras expect them to study the sacred writings of the Quran. Talibés also usually learn to read and write in Arabic, which are valuable skills in a nation where roughly half the adult population is illiterate.

Some of Senegal's daaras uphold the values on which the schools were founded. But at others, marabouts spend very little time, if any, teaching the boys in their care. Instead, they force them to beg—and to hand over all the money they gather. Experts estimate that at least fifty thousand Senegalese talibé children, some as young as four or five years old, are exploited by abusive marabouts. Many of these boys are injured or killed by cars as they wander the chaotic streets of Dakar, the nation's densely populated capital. Pape, a thirteen-year-old talibé, described such an accident. He said, "My friend—we begged together—was killed by a car. It happened when the sun was almost down, during the cold season. We were out begging and a car hit him. It was a big car. I don't know how it happened. The car just hit him and he died, right next to me."

Some marabouts forbid talibés to see or speak to their families. The boys often do not have enough to eat, and many are abused by the marabouts. To avoid punishment, each talibé must collect a certain amount of money or food each day. "If we don't get enough money, the marabout asks the older talibés to hold our hands and feet together while he beats us," says a boy named Ablaye. Another talibé, Ismaila, went to a daara when he was four years old and lived there for five years without ever seeing his family. He recalled, "[The marabout] asked us to bring rice, sugar and if ever we didn't bring anything, we were beaten severely. He used a *gourdin,* the club you use on sheep or goats." Other boys describe being chained to their beds overnight when they did not please their marabout. In addition, disease and other dangers can spread with terrifying speed through the cramped and dirty quarters where talibés live. One night in March 2013, fire broke out in a small Dakar house in which a marabout had locked at least forty boys. Nine talibés died.

FOR A FEW COINS

Child trafficking also includes children who are forced to beg for money. As is true for many victims of trafficking, these children are especially vulnerable to exploitation if they are members of an ethnic minority. In many parts of Europe, for example, a large proportion of forced child beggars are Roma (also called Romani, or gypsies). Roma live all over the world, with a high concentration in Europe, where they encounter discrimination and often live in extreme poverty. As a result, the Roma—and especially children—are vulnerable to trafficking, often by their fellow Roma.

Many forced child beggars have physical disabilities, which traffickers exploit. In Pakistan and Bangladesh, some traffickers abduct disabled children (and sometimes adults) from their homes and take them to other countries to force them to beg. Other traffickers in Bangladesh have been accused of abducting healthy children and then maiming them before sending them out to beg. These traffickers know that passersby—especially in nations with large numbers of tourists—are more likely to give money to disabled children. One report calculates that in Thailand, child beggars with some form of disability bring in an estimated three times more money than children without disabilities.

Impoverished ethnic minorities in any nation are vulnerable to exploitation. In this photo, a Somali child begs on the streets in Jeddah, a major urban center of western Saudi Arabia. Youth beggars on the streets anywhere in the world may be victims of human trafficking, forced to turn over their earnings to the traffickers who exploit them.

Human trafficking affects millions of families around the globe. This mother and child are in debt bondage at a Pakistani brick factory.

Our message today . . . is—to the millions [of trafficking victims] around the world—we see you. We hear you. We insist on your dignity. And we share your belief that if just given the chance, you will forge a life equal to your talents and worthy of your dreams.

—President Barack Obama, speaking to world leaders at a Clinton Global Initiative event, 2012

Human trafficking takes place in every nation of the world. It affects millions of people. Every country in the world has laws banning slavery. In addition to enacting laws, governments, organizations, and individuals continue to use a variety of approaches to battle human trafficking.

INTERNATIONAL PROBLEM, INTERNATIONAL RESPONSE

Because a significant portion of human trafficking involves moving people across international borders, nations around the world have come together to create international laws and treaties to direct the battle against human trafficking. For example, the United Nations enacted the Protocol to Prevent, Suppress, and Punish Trafficking in Persons, Especially Women and Children—also known as the Palermo Protocol—in 2000. This agreement, signed by more than 150 nations, requires member countries to protect victims of trafficking by taking steps such as enacting national laws against trafficking, shielding victims from deportation, and prosecuting traffickers with harsh penalties and prison sentences.

VOICES FOR CHANGE: RANI

Rani grew up in southern India. She was seven years old when her father became too sick to work. When a well-respected woman in a nearby village offered to take Rani as a servant, promising her a better life, Rani's parents agreed. Rani's mother thought she'd be able to visit her daughter every day. But as Rani recounts, "One day when she came to visit me, I was gone."

Rani's parents had unintentionally surrendered her into a trafficking network. At first, Rani didn't understand what had happened to her. "I cried and cried for my mom," she recalls. She also doesn't remember some of what happened during her captivity. The memories are too painful.

Rani does remember that when she was eight years old, her trafficker sold her into international adoption in the United States. It was an illegal adoption, but her new family was caring, and with time, Rani began to heal. She began to share what she could remember of her experiences. She says, "Telling my story is difficult. No one wants to relive that. But I know that I came through it, and I want to be a voice for those [other] voiceless

Some international agreements concentrate on specific segments of the human trafficking trade. For example, in 2001 an ambassador of the Ivory Coast, several US politicians, and representatives of major cocoa and chocolate companies—including M&M/Mars, Nestlé, and Hershey—signed the Harkin-Engel Protocol. This agreement is commonly called the Cocoa Protocol and aims to eliminate trafficked child labor in the cocoa-farming industry. The protocol calls for the chocolate industry to set up industry-wide standards to end the use of child labor and to inform consumers about labor practices in cocoa farming.

On a broader scale, the International Labour Organization has a mission to uphold the rights of workers around the world. Part of this mission includes fighting labor trafficking through enforcement of laws,

children." She began to think of ways to help others. She asked herself, "How do we prevent this from happening to another mother, and another child?"

Rani Hong now lives in Olympia, Washington. With her husband, Trong Hong, she founded the Tronie Foundation. The foundation set up a shelter in Olympia, giving survivors of various types of trafficking a safe and welcoming place to live. It also offers job training and other support. The Tronie Foundation also works with companies to educate employees about trafficking issues.

In addition to working with her foundation, Rani has served as a special adviser to the United Nations Global Initiative to Fight Human Trafficking. In this role, she advocates for the victims of trafficking around the world.

Another of Rani's projects is a campaign called Rani's Voice, which encourages former victims to speak out about their experiences and to become leaders in the fight against human trafficking. Rani says of her mission, "The goal of the campaign is to spread the message of survivors' voices, because when you partner with me . . . you are letting us know our voice is important."

prosecution of traffickers, and identification of victims. Similarly, the International Organization for Migration (IOM) has an overarching goal of protecting the legal and human rights of migrants and combats trafficking as part of this mission.

National laws and international treaties against human trafficking make a statement. Yet unless they're enforced and those who break them are punished, these measures make little difference in the long run. Enforcement has proven to be a challenge. Sometimes countries don't have the resources to track down and catch traffickers—or governments and law enforcement are complicit in trafficking. In other cases, police officers and other officials are not trained to recognize the signs and victims of trafficking. Additionally, even when traffickers are taken to court, inadequate evidence often mars the cases against them. The United Nations estimates that in 2006, fewer than 6,000 prosecutions and only 3,160 convictions of human trafficking crimes were achieved globally. According to some estimates, that is only about one conviction for every eight hundred people trafficked.

THE UNITED STATES AND BEYOND

The US government has put in place a number of laws and programs that confront human trafficking. In 2000 the United States enacted the Victims of Trafficking and Violence Protection Act. The law was renewed and updated in 2003, 2005, and 2008. Under these laws, some immigrant victims who can prove that they've been trafficked and who agree to testify against the traffickers are legally allowed to stay and work in the United States on special visas.

In 2003 the US Department of Justice also started a program called the Innocence Lost National Initiative, a joint initiative with the FBI and the National Center for Missing and Exploited Children (NCMEC). Innocence Lost focuses on the sex trafficking of children in the United States. The initiative's work includes training state and federal law officers to identify and aid potential victims. In addition, the initiative spearheads

A GUIDING STAR

The Polaris Project is one of many organizations working to fight trafficking. It is named after the North Star. During the era of slavery in the United States, slaves escaping captivity in the southern part of the country followed a route known as the Underground Railroad. They used the bright North Star to help them find their way to freedom in the North and in Canada. Polaris was founded in 2002 by Katherine Chon and Derek Ellerman. At the time, Chon and Ellerman were recent university graduates who had learned about the extent of human trafficking during their senior year of college.

The Polaris Project is based in Washington, DC, and works for stronger anti-trafficking laws and better enforcement of them. The project also provides victims of trafficking with legal advocacy assistance, therapy, and a wide variety of workshops to help victims adjust to life after they have been freed. In addition, the project runs the National Human Trafficking Resource Center hotline for citizens to report suspected trafficking and for victims to call for help. Callers to the hotline can also learn more about how to fight trafficking in their area. In 2012 the Polaris Project launched an initiative called Vision 2020, which aims, in part, to establish trafficking hotlines around the world.

law enforcement actions such as Operation Cross Country. Carried out over three days in July 2013, this sting operation brought together officers from the FBI and from local and state levels. It targeted seventy-six cities and resulted in the rescue of more than one hundred sexually exploited children, as well as the arrest of 152 pimps. Since its founding, Innocence Lost has led to the rescue of more than twenty-seven hundred children.

Within the United States, individual states and cities take steps to fight human trafficking. In 2013 alone, forty-seven US states enacted 186 bills addressing the trafficking of minors into the sex trade. Shared Hope International, an anti-sex-trafficking organization based in Washington

State, gives states a grade each year for their efforts in eradicating sex trafficking. In 2013 Tennessee received the highest grade. The state's strengths included serious penalties for people convicted of trafficking and also for people who assist traffickers. States also target labor trafficking. Virginia, for example, has enacted a law allowing authorities to bring charges of abduction against traffickers who force victims to do any kind of work.

In addition to these efforts at home, the United States has worked to identify the scope of the problem in individual nations around the world. In its annual *Trafficking in Persons (TIP) Report,* the US State Department ranks countries (including the United States) according to how effectively they are fighting trafficking. The *TIP* sorts nations into three tiers. Tier 1 nations, though not completely free of trafficking, have "acknowledged the existence of human trafficking, [have] made efforts to address the problem, and meet . . . minimum standards." Those standards include enacting and enforcing laws against trafficking and working to identify and aid victims. In 2013 countries in Tier 1 included Australia, Belgium, Colombia, Germany, Israel, Italy, the Netherlands, Nicaragua, Poland, South Korea, the United Kingdom, and the United States.

Tier 2 countries are making significant efforts to combat trafficking within their borders. Tier 2 also includes a watch list of countries that have previously been at the Tier 2 level but are seeing an increase in trafficking or are otherwise at risk of falling into Tier 3. Tier 2 includes Argentina, Guatemala, India, Jamaica, Laos, Latvia, Moldova, Niger, Switzerland, and Uganda. The Tier 2 watch list includes Afghanistan, Angola, Cambodia, Haiti, Kenya, Lebanon, Rwanda, South Sudan, Thailand, and Ukraine.

Tier 3 nations do not comply with legal requirements and have not shown that they are taking major steps to do so. They include Algeria, China, Cuba, the Democratic Republic of the Congo, Iran, North Korea, Saudi Arabia, Sudan, Syria, and Zimbabwe. Some Tier 3 nations are embroiled in war or other conflicts that prevent them from effectively targeting trafficking. Other nations have corrupt governments or histories of human rights abuses and refuse to comply with international standards. In some cases, governments in poor nations are reluctant to shut down industries fueled by human trafficking because they bring in desperately needed profits in which corrupt government officials often share.

SLAVE REDEMPTION

Another response to trafficking is slave redemption—buying trafficked victims from owners and traders. In most cases, the buyers come from the United States or Europe and are members of churches or other organizations that have raised money for redemption missions. Slave redemption has happened primarily in Sudan and South Sudan. In this part of the world, groups such as Christian Solidarity International typically communicate with local slave traders and agree to meet and buy slaves for around thirty-five to fifty dollars each. These groups then returned the slaves to their homes and families.

A group of slaves in Sudan await their release. A human rights group called Christian Solidarity International arranged and paid for their freedom. The practice of slave redemption is controversial, as many experts believe that it may encourage some traffickers who hope to reap the profits of redemption.

This approach may seem like one of the most immediate and effective ways to deal with the issue of trafficking, since it directly frees individuals held in bondage. However, the practice is controversial. Some experts believe that it encourages traffickers by giving them the expectation of large payments for slaves they have kidnapped or coerced. Some slaveholders who might otherwise have released slaves who became too expensive to feed or house have a reason to keep them in hopes of earning money from "redeemers." In some cases, people have perpetrated hoaxes on redemption groups by selling them fake slaves. They simply round up people to pose as slaves and share the profits.

FROM THE GROUND UP

Around the world, many people are founding small, local organizations that fight trafficking one person at a time. For instance, in Thailand, Annie Dieselberg founded a group called NightLight to aid women who have been sex trafficked escape their situations. She visits the bars and clubs of Bangkok and forms relationships with the girls and women who work there, urging them to gather the courage to leave and to come to NightLight. As part of NightLight, former sex trafficking victims are hired to make jewelry, and they also receive education in other job and life skills.

In Spain MATTOO (Men Against the Trafficking of Others) works to foster greater respect for women and to educate boys and men about the connections between the sex trade and trafficking. In Dakar, Senegal, a group of neighborhood women have come together to help mistreated talibés. The women offer the boys meals, wash their clothes, help them with their learning, and provide them with a safe space to spend time. As Thioro Fall, one of these women, says, "If every household in Senegal helped a talibé like this, the number of children begging would decrease. One household, one talibé." And in Gulu, Uganda, the Children of War Rehabilitation Center provides safe shelter, medical care, and counseling for former child soldiers. The center also works to reunite these children with their families.

SEEING THE SIGNS

International agreements and national laws are critical in the fight against trafficking. But it's also important for individuals to learn how to recognize the signs of trafficking. Many people have passed trafficking victims on the street—or even had conversations with them—without realizing it. For instance, writer and professor David Batstone describes how he interacted with trafficked workers without having any idea that they were not working voluntarily. He says, "For several years my wife and I dined regularly at an Indian restaurant near our home in the San Francisco Bay area. Unbeknownst to us, the staff . . . who cooked our curries, delivered them to our table, and washed our dishes were slaves."

Signs that a person may have been trafficked include these:

- The person has no form of identification.
- The person has no cash or credit cards.
- The person is accompanied by someone who speaks for him or her.
- The person seems lost or afraid.
- The person has bruises or other signs of physical abuse.
- The person seems hungry or undernourished.

If you suspect that someone has been trafficked, it is never safe to approach the person or the possible trafficker. Instead, you can call organizations such as the US National Human Trafficking Resource Center hotline (1-888-373-7888) or text the center at BeFree (233733) to report what you have seen. By speaking up, you might make the difference between freedom and enslavement for a victim of human trafficking.

WHAT YOU CAN DO

Human trafficking is not a new phenomenon that affects only a small number of people or a select group of countries. It is a complex, global challenge. Yet every person can help in the fight against modern slavery. Being aware of the problem—and how close to home it can be—is an important step. For example, do you know who made the clothes you wear? Who farms and processes the food you eat? Do you know who works behind the scenes at your favorite restaurant? Many of the people we rely on in our daily lives and the things we use every day may be the products of trafficked labor. According to Anti-Slavery International, 122 products in fifty-eight countries are produced through forced labor. These goods include agricultural products such as chocolate, cotton, spices, rice, and sugarcane. They also include manufactured items such as shoes, clothes, jewelry, electronics, and furniture.

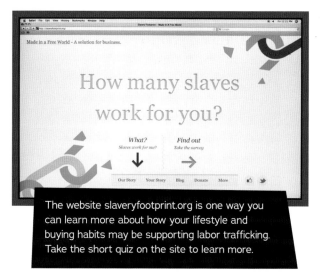

The website slaveryfootprint.org is one way you can learn more about how your lifestyle and buying habits may be supporting labor trafficking. Take the short quiz on the site to learn more.

At slaveryfootprint.org, you can take a survey that estimates how your habits and lifestyle may support modern-day slavery. You can follow up by learning more about the link between human trafficking and specific products and nations at Anti-Slavery's website productsofslavery.org. The site offers ideas for how to make more informed consumer decisions so you can say no to global slavery.

As a next step, you can research individual companies. For example, visit the website free2work.org to learn more about specific brands of clothing, electronic goods, and more. If and when you find out about company practices that support human trafficking, you can choose not to buy that company's products. You can decide to spend your money instead on items you know were not produced by slave labor. You can also contact offending companies by e-mail to voice your concerns. Write letters to the editor at your local newspaper to spread the word. Contact your local or state representatives and urge them to join the fight by supporting anti-trafficking laws and working for the enforcement of existing policies.

Share what you've learned with family, friends, and classmates. Hold a fund-raiser at school or in your community, and donate the money you raise to an anti-trafficking organization you like. Young people around the world have started small, with big ideas—from organizing fund-raising walks, to setting up a Free Trade club at school to raise awareness about the cocoa industry and the chocolate we eat, to attending youth summits and pledging to educate others.

Human trafficking does not have simple causes, and it does not have simple solutions. But you can take meaningful action on an individual level to fight modern-day slavery, and you can encourage others to do the same. Everyone has the power to work toward a future in which people are not up for sale.

"The problem of modern trafficking may be entrenched, and it may seem like there is no end in sight. But if we act on the laws that have been passed and the commitments that have been made, it is solvable."

—Hillary Rodham Clinton, US secretary of state, 2011

Source Notes

4   David Batstone, *Not for Sale: The Return of the Global Slave Trade—and How We Can Fight It* (New York: HarperCollins, 2010), 1.

5   US Department of State, *Trafficking in Persons Report 2013,* June 2013, accessed November 1, 2013, http://www.state.gov/j/tip/rls/tiprpt/2013.

11 United Nations, "The Universal Declaration of Human Rights," December 10, 1948, accessed May 12, 2013, http://www.un.org/en/documents/udhr.

12 Jesse Sage and Liora Kasten, eds., *Enslaved: True Stories of Modern Day Slavery* (New York: Palgrave MacMillan, 2008), 49.

13 Sam Dillon, "Conflicting View Emerges of Family Linked to Deaf," *New York Times,* July 23, 1997, accessed October 4, 2013, http://www.nytimes.com/1997/07/23/nyregion /conflicting-view-emerges-of-family-linked-to-deaf.html.

13 Joseph Goldstein, "Two Plead Guilty in Decade-Old Slavery Case," *New York Sun,* June 29, 2006, accessed October 4, 2013, http://www.nysun.com/new-york/two-plead-guilty-in -decade-old-slavery-case/35266.

13 Joseph P. Fried, "2 Sentenced in Mexican Peddling Ring," *New York Times,* May 8, 1998, accessed October 5, 2013, http://www.nytimes.com/1998/05/08/nyregion/2-sentenced-in -mexican-peddling-ring.html.

13 Dillon, "Conflicting View."

13 Ibid.

14 Tim Golden and Ian Fisher, "For Deaf Peddlers, Both Opportunity and Exploitation," *New York Times,* July 27, 1997, accessed October 4, 2013, http://www.nytimes.com/1997/07/27 /nyregion/for-deaf-peddlers-both-opportunity-and-exploitation.html.

15 Amnesty International, *False Promises: Exploitation and Forced Labour of Nepalese Migrant Workers,* accessed May 26, 2013, http://globalsentrygroup.files.wordpress .com/2012/12/english-nepal-mw-report1.pdf.

17 "Open Letter to Attorney General Eric Holder from Thai Workers Impacted by Federal Government's Decision to Drop Labor Trafficking Charges against Global Horizons Principals," *Hawaii Reporter,* August 13, 2012, accessed April 23, 2013, http://www .hawaiireporter.com/open-letter-to-attorney-general-eric-holder-from-thai-workers-impacted -by-federal-governments-decision-to-drop-labor-trafficking-charges-against-global-horizons -principals/123.

18 Anthony M. DeStefano, *The War on Human Trafficking: U.S. Policy Assessed* (New Brunswick, NJ: Rutgers University Press, 2008), 70.

19 David Gonzalez, "When American Dream Leads to Servitude," *New York Times,* April 24, 2007, accessed November 7, 2013, http://www.nytimes.com/2007/04/24/nyregion /24citywide.html.

20 US Department of State, *Trafficking in Persons Report 2012,* June 2012, accessed June 2, 2013, http://www.state.gov/j/tip/rls/tiprpt/2012.

21 Anti-Slavery, "Bonded Labor," accessed May 10, 2013, http://www.antislavery.org/english
    /slavery_today/bonded_labour.aspx.

22 Beate Andrees, "Forced Labour and Trafficking in Europe: How People Are Trapped In,
    Live Through, and Come Out" (Geneva: International Labour Organization, 2008), 11.

22 Kevin Bales, *Disposable People: New Slavery in the Global Economy* (Berkeley: University
    of California Press, 2012), 206.

23 Ibid., 218.

26 "Outrage at 'Slavery' in Bolivia," *BBC News,* May 14, 2009, accessed June 14, 2013, http://
    news.bbc.co.uk/2/hi/americas/8047960.stm.

29 "Illegal Organ Deals Strike Fear into Chinese Hearts," *China Daily,* June 8, 2011, accessed
    July 1, 2013, http://www.chinadaily.com.cn/china/2011-06/08/content_12659079.htm.

29 Dan Bilefsky, "Black Market for Body Parts Spreads among the Poor in Europe," *New York
    Times,* June 28, 2012, accessed July 1, 2013, http://www.nytimes.com/2012/06/29/world
    /europe/black-market-for-body-parts-spreads-in-europe.html.

30 US Department of State, *Trafficking in Persons Report 2013.*

31 DeStefano, *The War on Human Trafficking,* 3.

33 Victor Malarek, *The Natashas: The New Global Sex Trade* (New York: Viking, 2003), 113.

33–34 Chiara Caprio, "Italian and Nigerian Gangs: A Deadly Alliance," *Independent* (London),
    September 27, 2011, accessed June 26, 2013, http://www.independent.co.uk/news/world
    -and-nigerian-gangs-a-deadly-alliance-2361393.html.

34 Melissa Farley, Nicole Matthews, Sarah Deer, Guadalupe Lopez, Christine Stark, and Eileen
    Hudon, *Garden of Truth: The Prostitution and Trafficking of Native Women in Minnesota,*
    October 27, 2011, accessed June 19, 2013, http://www.prostitutionresearch.com/pdfs
    /Garden_of_Truth_Final_Project_WEB.pdf.

35 US Department of State, *Trafficking in Persons Report 2012.*

35 Nicholas D. Kristof, "Not Quite a Teen, Yet Sold for Sex," *New York Times,* April 18, 2012,
    accessed April 29, 2013, http://www.nytimes.com/2012/04/19/opinion/kristof-not-quite-a
    -teen-yet-sold-for-sex.html.

37 "Transcript of Sentencing before the Honorable James C. Cacheris," *United States of
    America vs. Justin Deonta Strom,* September 14, 2012, accessed June 4, 2013, http://
    s3.documentcloud.org/documents/605417/strom-sentencing-transcript-091412.pdf.

38 Ibid.

38 Justin Jouvenal, "Underage Prostitution Ring's Leader Sentenced to 40 Years in Prison,"
    Washington Post, September 14, 2012, accessed November 1, 2013, http://articles
    .washingtonpost.com/2012-09-14/local/35496088_1_underground-gangster-crips-justin
    -strom-underage-girl.

38 "Transcript of Sentencing before the Honorable James C. Cacheris," *United States of America vs. Justin Deonta Strom.*

39 Polaris Project, "Internet Based," accessed June 18, 2013, http://www.polarisproject.org /human-trafficking/sex-trafficking-in-the-us/internet-based.

40 US Department of Homeland Security, "ICE Most Wanted Fugitive Arrested at JFK on Human Trafficking Charges," January 27, 2011, accessed July 9, 2013, http://www.ice.gov /news/releases/1101/110127detroit.htm.

42 "Hidden Slaves: Forced Labor in the United States," *Berkeley Journal of International Law* 23, no. 1 (2005), accessed June 11, 2013, http://scholarship.law.berkeley.edu/bjil/vol23 /iss1/2.

43 "Uganda Attempts to End Decades' Long Civil War," *PBS Newshour,* April 26, 2007, accessed July 8, 2013, http://www.pbs.org/newshour/bb/africa/jan-june07/uganda_04-26 .htm.

44 Heather Sells, "Sex Tourists: Brazil Fights 'Out of Control' Child Exploitation," *CBN News,* March 1, 2013, accessed November 10, 2013, http://www.cbn.com/cbnnews/world/2012 /July/Brazils-Sex-Trafficked-Kids-Caught-in-Web-of-Crime.

45 Michael Wessells, *Child Soldiers: From Violence to Prevention* (Cambridge, MA: Harvard University Press, 2009), 63.

46 Ibid., 39.

47 Andrew Jacobs, "Chinese Hunger for Sons Fuels Boys' Abductions," *New York Times,* April 4, 2009, accessed June 4, 2013, http//:www.nytimes.com/2009/04/05/world/asia /05kidnap.html.

49 E. J. Graff, "The Lie We Love: Foreign Adoption Seems Like a Win-Win Arrangement. Unfortunately, Those Bundles of Joy May Not Be Orphans at All," *Utne,* May–June 2009, accessed June 5, 2013, http://www.utne.com/Politics/International-Adoption-Lies-Orphans -Myths.aspx?PageId=3#axzz2kJD9Eq8v.

51 Human Rights Watch, *"Off the Backs of Children": Forced Begging and Other Abuses against Talibés in Senegal,* accessed June 2, 2013, http://www.hrw.org/sites/default/files /reports/senegal0410webwcover.pdf.

51 Misha Hussalin, "Senegalese Children Forced to Beg by Renegade Teachers' Betrayal of Principle," *Guardian* (London), December 11, 2012, accessed June 2, 2013, http://www .guardian.co.uk/global-development/2012/dec/11/senegalese-children-forced-beg-renegade -teachers.

51 Angus Crawford, "Senegal School Abuse: Ismaila's Story," *BBC News,* September 15, 2010, accessed June 2, 2013, http://www.bbc.co.uk/news/world-africa-11265339.

53 The White House, "Remarks by the President to the Clinton Global Initiative," September 25, 2012, accessed May 2, 2013, http://www.whitehouse.gov/the-press-office/2012/09/25 /remarks-president-clinton-global-initiative.

54 "Rani Hong's Story," *YouTube*, 2:48, posted by Rani Hong, December 21, 2010, accessed June 9, 2013, http://www.youtube.com/watch?v=s_hruXnwAfE.

54 Ibid.

54–55 Christina Fisanick, ed., *Human Trafficking* (Detroit: Greenhaven Press, 2010), 69.

55 "Transcripts: Connect the World," *CNN*, November 4, 2010, accessed June 9, 2013, http://edition.cnn.com/TRANSCRIPTS/1011/04/ctw.01.html.

55 "Rani's Voice: Human Rights Day 2011," *YouTube*, 2:11, posted by Rani Hong, December 8, 2011, accessed June 9, 2013, http://www.youtube.com/watch?v=YTZq8Fh1n74.

58 US Department of State, *Trafficking in Persons Report 2013.*

60 IRIN, "Senegal: One Household, 'One Talibé,'" October 8, 2010, accessed June 3, 2013, http://www.irinnews.org/report.aspx?reportid=.

61 Batstone, *Not for Sale,* 1.

63 US Department of State, *Trafficking in Persons Report 2012.*

Selected Bibliography

Bales, Kevin, and Steven Lize. *Trafficking in Persons in the United States: A Report to the National Institute of Justice.* August 2005. Accessed May 10, 2013. http://www.freetheslaves.net /Document.Doc?id=12.

Bales, Kevin, and Ron Soodalter. *The Slave Next Door: Human Trafficking and Slavery in America Today.* Berkeley: University of California Press, 2009.

Carney, Scott. *The Red Market: On the Trail of the World's Organ Brokers, Bone Thieves, Blood Farmers, and Child Traffickers.* New York: William Morrow, 2011.

DeStefano, Anthony M. *The War on Human Trafficking: U.S. Policy Assessed.* New Brunswick, NJ: Rutgers University Press, 2008.

European Roma Rights Centre and People in Need. *Breaking the Silence: Trafficking in Romani Communities.* March 2011. Accessed April 30, 2013. http://www.errc.org/cms/upload/file /breaking-the-silence-19-march-2011.pdf.

Harroff-Tavel, Hélène, and Alix Nasri. *Tricked and Trapped: Human Trafficking in the Middle East.* Accessed May 17, 2013. http://www.ilo.org/wcmsp5/groups/public/---arabstates/---ro-beirut /documents/publication/wcms_211214.pdf.

International Labour Organization. *Training Manual to Fight Trafficking in Children for Labour, Sexual and Other Forms of Exploitation: Understanding Child Trafficking.* Accessed June 2, 2013. http://www.unicef.org/protection/Textbook_1.pdf.

Kara, Siddharth. *Sex Trafficking: Inside the Business of Modern Slavery.* New York: Columbia University Press, 2009.

Lloyd, Rachel. *Girls Like Us: Fighting for a World Where Girls Are Not for Sale: A Memoir.* New York: Harper Perennial, 2011.

OSCE/Office of the Special Representative and Coordinator for Combating Trafficking in Human Beings. *Unprotected Work, Invisible Exploitation: Trafficking for the Purpose of Domestic Servitude.* Accessed June 2, 2013. http://www.osce.org/cthb/75804.

Shelley, Louise. *Human Trafficking: A Global Perspective.* New York: Cambridge University Press, 2010.

Skinner, E. Benjamin. *A Crime So Monstrous: Face-to-Face with Modern-Day Slavery.* New York: Free Press, 2008.

United Nations Office on Drugs and Crime. *Global Report on Trafficking in Persons 2012.* Accessed June 2, 2013. http://www.unodc.org/documents/data-and-analysis/glotip/Trafficking_in_ Persons_2012_web.pdf.

——. *Human Trafficking: An Overview.* Accessed July 14, 2013. http://www.ungift.org/docs /ungift/pdf/knowledge/ebook.pdf.

For Further Information

Books

Beah, Ihmael. *A Long Way Gone: Memoirs of a Boy Soldier.* New York: Farrar, Straus and Giroux, 2007. In this true account, Beah tells his story of life as a child soldier in Sierra Leone in West Africa.

D'Adamo, Francesco. *Iqbal.* Translated by Ann Lenori. New York: Atheneum, 2003. This novel tells a fictionalized version of the true story of Iqbal Masih, a teenage activist who exposed the reality of child labor in Pakistan—and who was murdered for his courage.

Haerens, Margaret, ed. *Human Trafficking.* Global Viewpoints series. Detroit: Greenhaven Press, 2012. This collection of articles explores various aspects of human trafficking, including nation-specific situations, factors that contribute to trafficking around the world, and strategies for addressing the problem.

Hepburn, Stephanie, and Rita J. Simon. *Human Trafficking around the World: Hidden in Plain Sight.* New York: Columbia University Press, 2013. This book takes a hard look at the many forms of human trafficking and exploitation, from organ trafficking to sex tourism.

Kristof, Nicholas, and Sheryl WuDunn. *Half the Sky: Turning Oppression into Opportunity for Women Worldwide.* New York: Alfred A. Knopf, 2009. This book explores a range of ways women and girls are mistreated around the globe, including child sex trafficking in India.

Mam, Somaly. With Ruth Marshall. *The Road of Lost Innocence: The True Story of a Cambodian Heroine.* New York: Spiegel & Grau, 2008. Somaly Mam, a survivor of child sex trafficking in Cambodia, tells her story in this memoir.

McCormick, Patricia. *Sold.* New York: Hyperion, 2006. This YA novel tells the fictionalized tale of a young Nepalese girl trafficked into prostitution.

Nazer, Mende, and Damien Lewis. *Slave: My True Story.* New York: Public Affairs, 2003. At the age of twelve, Mende Nazer was kidnapped during a slave raid in Sudan and sold as a slave to a wealthy family. In this book, she describes her experiences.

Newman, Shirlee P. *Child Slavery in Modern Times.* New York: Franklin Watts, 2000. This book takes a look at child victims of human trafficking.

Purcell, Kim. *Trafficked.* New York: Viking, 2012. This novel follows the story of Hannah, a teenager from Moldova who agrees to become a nanny in Los Angeles—and soon discovers that she's been ensnared by slavery.

Sage, Jesse, and Liora Kasten, eds. *Enslaved: True Stories of Modern Day Slavery.* New York: Palgrave MacMillan, 2008. This book tells the true stories of modern-day slaves around the world, from Sudan to China to the United States.

Schlimm, John. *Stand Up! 75 Young Activists Who Rock the World and How You Can, Too!* Orangevale, CA: Publishing Syndicate, 2013. This book introduces the efforts of dozens of kids and teens who have taken action to confront and solve problems including human trafficking.

Websites

Coalition Against Trafficking in Women (CATW)
http://www.catwinternational.org
Founded in 1988, CATW is an international organization that speaks up for women, children, and others who have been trafficked and works to end exploitation by lobbying governments, supporting victims, and educating others on the issue.

Free the Slaves
http://www.freetheslaves.net
This nonprofit organization is based in the United States and works to end slavery around the globe.

Global Alliance Against Traffic in Women (GAATW)
http://gaatw.com
Headquartered in Bangkok, Thailand, GAATW is an alliance of more than one hundred nongovernmental organizations. By sharing information about trafficking and urging local and national governments to support human rights, GAATW works to fight human trafficking around the world.

La Strada International
http://lastradainternational.org
This European network, comprised of eight nations—mostly in eastern Europe—has a mission to fight trafficking of persons to, from, and within Europe.

NASHI
http://nashi.ca
This Canada-based organization works to fight human trafficking by raising awareness among youth and others. The group also runs a center in Ukraine, working to fight trafficking there.

The Polaris Project
http://www.polarisproject.org
This organization works to educate others about human trafficking and to fight the problem in the United States and around the world.

Slavery Footprint
http://slaveryfootprint.org
A simple survey on this website helps visitors understand how their habits and lifestyle impact human trafficking around the world. The site offers practical tips on how to live in a way that has a smaller trafficking footprint.

Index

About the Author

Alison Marie Behnke is a writer and editor. She has written about and researched a wide range of topics and in a variety of genres, including immigration, world and cultural geography, ethnic cuisines, American and European history, biographies, and fashion. Her books include *Death of a Dreamer: The Assassination of John Lennon, The Conquests of Alexander the Great,* and *Kim Jong Il's North Korea.* She also loves to travel, and her travels have brought her face-to-face with evidence of human trafficking. This exposure drew her to learn more about trafficking around the world—and what can be done to end it. She lives in Minneapolis.

Photo Acknowledgments

The images in this book are used with the permission of: backgrounds © Pokaz/Bigstock.com; © JF Leblanc/Alamy, p. 4; © DEA/G. Dagli/DeAgostini/Getty Images, p. 6; AP Photo/ImagineChina, p. 7; © Roger Huchings/Alamy, p. 9; © Fotosearch/Archive Photos/Getty Images, p. 11; AP Photo/ Carlos Villalon, p. 12; © Juanmonino/E+/Getty Images, p. 15; AP Photo/Ric Francis, p. 20; AP Photo/Altaf Qadri, p. 23; © Yusuf Ahmad/Reuters/CORBIS, p. 25; © Mario Tama/Getty Images, p. 26; AP Photo/K.M.Chaudary, p. 27; REUTERS/Andrew Biraj, p. 30; © iStockphoto.com/Gremlin, p. 32; © Gideon Mendel/CORBIS, p. 40; AP Photo/Spanish Police, p. 41; © Kevin Foy/Alamy, p. 43; © REUTERS, p. 46; AP Photo/Moises Castillo, p. 48; © Friedrich Stark/Alamy, p. 50; © Eric Lafforgue/arabianEye/CORBIS, p. 52; © Imagebroker/Alamy, p. 53; © Reuters/CORBIS, p. 59; Courtesy of Independent Picture Service, p. 62.

Front cover: © Lawrence Manning/CORBIS (main); Pokaz/Bigstock.com (background).

Main body text set in Gamma ITC Std 11/15. Typeface provided by International Typeface Corp.